7 Secrets Commercial Cleaning Companies Don't Want You To Know

Office Cleaning Is More Than Dusting and Vacuuming

Christopher Banner

Published by Keystone Vortex Publishing, Albuquerque, New Mexico

Banner, Christopher

7 Secrets Cleaning Companies Don't Want You To Know / Christopher Banner

ISBN 978-0-9889662-3-9

PRINTED IN THE UNITED STATES OF AMERICA

First Edition

Table of Contents

About The Author
Christopher Banner

Christopher Banner is the President & CEO of Bright Star Cleaning, a commercial office cleaning company based in Albuquerque, New Mexico that provides services to many in the medical industry and other special needs companies.

Christopher was born in London and lived there for most of his life. He began his career in the corporate financial services world and rose through the ranks of several large British corporations. Certified by Chartered Institute of Management Accounts, he trained as a Financial Accounting Professional and advanced to CFO of the Financial Times Business Information Division (the Wall Street Journal of Great Britain) and Thomson Reuters Publishing. He obtained the British designation for professional accounting equivalent to the American CPA certification.

A few years later, he and a partner built a new company providing critical industry information to large corporate entities in Great Britain. Together, they built that company into a $20 Million firm at the top of its game in England and then sold the company.

In 2005 he moved to New Mexico with his wife and infant daughter. After several years of semi-retirement Chris purchased an existing commercial cleaning company because of his desire to bring an English Butler style White Glove cleaning improvement to the commercial cleaning industry.

Introduction

The office cleaning industry is a hodge-podge assortment of companies with little or no industry oversight.

That means that almost anyone can hang out a shingle and call themselves a commercial cleaning company.

Because of this low threshold to entry, you are likely to receive less than stellar systematic cleaning service. And sometimes the people getting into the business do not have the good business sense for running a cleaning company.

Not only that, several of the large national companies are only selling by price and cutting quality of service.

How can you protect yourself?

In this book I have taken time to reveal several of the failings in our industry that you need to protect yourself and your business against.

There are conditions in this industry that attract people whose only motive is to start a business and make a bunch of money.

This also drives them to cut corners. You'll notice they seldom have a specific system for cleaning that insures a professional cleaning job.

You need to protect your company, your employees and your customers, clients or patients from poor quality cleaning.

You can do that by familiarizing yourself with some of the shocking secrets that crop up in our industry. You can also following some of safeguards I've outlined in this book to make it easier for you.

Chapter 1

They Think They Can Be Everything To Everybody

Often you will find cleaning companies that start out cleaning homes and suddenly decide, "we can do offices too".

They incorrectly decide, "if we can clean someone's private residence we can clean offices and make more money."

That almost sounds logical right, at least it does to the home cleaning business owner. B-U-T, you don't conduct business in your home...usually.

Christopher Banner

If the cleaning company you are considering also cleans houses, I recommend passing and looking for a professional office cleaning company.

Why is that?

There is a significant difference in the cleaning needs and requirements for an office and the cleaning elements of a home.

FIRST, your office represents your company.

Prospects, customers, patients, clients and vendors have a tendency to make snap judgments about your company based on their perception of your offices.

This is especially so when it comes to healthcare facility offices.

If you go into your dentist and the waiting room has dust bunnies in the corner, what will you think about the germ free nature of his surgeries?

Or, if you walk in the restroom of a medical practice and there are no paper towels to dry your hands, what is your perception of the state of his medical supplies used in your diagnosis?

Often these thoughts are subconscious. You'll think to yourself, there is something hinky about this place, but you just can't put your finger on it.

Ray Kroc And McDonalds

Ray Kroc was the visionary that created the national behemoth that is the McDonald's Franchise industry.

He once told a group of his franchisees the following story.

"Kids can't tell the difference between the quality of one cheeseburger or another but mothers would always know and remember which bathrooms were clean and which weren't."

"A clean bathroom is marketing," he declared emphatically.

Your business is always on display. People are constantly making judgments about your company, about your staff from the atmosphere they feel in your offices.

If your business is in the healthcare industry, medical practice, dental office, physical therapy, periodontist, orthodontics, chiropractic, natural healing or other health care provider, your income and the number of patients you can help, can easily be tied to the look and feel of your office and treatment rooms.

A friend of mine told me this story.

"I once went to a new dentist in Albuquerque. As I was sitting and waiting for the dentist to look at my teeth, I got this uneasy feeling about the place."

"As you can probably understand, I'm not especially excited about going to see the dentist in the first place."

"But for some reason I just didn't feel right about this place. I quickly made an excuse that I had forgotten about an appointment I had. I left in a hurry to get out of the place."

"Later as I was analyzing my reaction, I realized what caused me to bolt from the appointment."

"When I was in the waiting room, I could see into the office manager's office. There were stacks of paper everywhere. Cardboard file boxes were stacked half way up the wall."

"I had also subconsciously noted that the dental supply cabinet was open and the items inside were in disarray."

"Until I analyzed it later, I wasn't really aware of it at the time, but the state of the office impacted my opinion of the rest of the dentist care."

The same will happen with your prospects, customers, visitors and vendors.

Since these people supply the lifeblood to your business (sales and money), the last thing you should be thinking about is finding ways to shortcut your office cleaning bill.

I'm not suggesting that you just throw a lot of money away on a cleaning company.

You should see your cleaning company as a partner. Invite them in and use them as an expert resource and fresh set of eyes.

Have them look at your office from a customer's perspective and give you recommendations on those things that should be done.

You need a professional cleaning organization that specializes in cleaning offices. If they clean houses too, they often will not have the expertise to help you analyze your needs.

A cleaning company that says they do everything will often miss the things that are needed for a professional office environment.

I'll be talking about some of those later in this book.

After all, you know the old saying: "Jack of all Trades and Master of None".

This is very true when it comes to cleaning companies.

You should never trust your office cleaning to a 'Jack of all Trades'.

A Sparkling Clean Office IS Marketing

Or another mistake I see made is one another friend of mine experienced when he visited the showroom of an RV dealership.

They were selling $50,000 plus travel trailers and $100,000 to $500,000 RV motor homes. When he walked in, the large throw rug in the waiting room was frayed around the edges, musty smelling and dirty.

Cobwebs were noticeable in two of the corners of the salespersons office.

There were large florescent light fixtures in the ceiling that were full of dead bugs. My friend didn't buy from that dealer. He told me he was concerned they would treat his RV the same way.

(By the way, we invented a special system for cleaning bugs out of our client's light fixtures that we are awaiting patent approval at this time.)

Later he found out the dealership had hired one of their employees to moonlight and do the cleaning to make some extra money.

I'll bet this saved the dealership a lot of money on cleaning bills.

However, that employee was hired for their skills in the office, not their skills at cleaning. On top of that, cleaning wasn't that employee's first priority or training. She did just enough to get by when it came to cleaning.

And the dealer missed at least one sale from my friend because of it. I bet it was a lot more

Chapter 2

Bait & Switch

Bait and Switch, that is an ugly term isn't it? But I'm afraid it is happening all too often in our industry.

Here's the problem. Many of the largest commercial cleaning companies have an army of sales people on the phone making appointments.

Or, they are out walking the streets going into every building and business door begging for an appointment to switch out the cleaning company.

What causes this?

The sales people and the companies only know how to interest you in their service by promising a lower price.

And who wouldn't want to reduce some costs. The truth is you may be a little dissatisfied with your current Company A. And, you can often look like a hero by cutting expenses like these.

So you agree to getting the same level of service for a lower price from the new Company B. That seems like a smart decision.

With competition price often does comes down.

But think of your industry. Does just dropping the price improve the quality of the products or services in your industry?

No! You know this intuitively.

The only way you can use competition to lower prices and still have the same or better quality is through innovation.

And, those price dropping cleaning companies are not using innovation to create better pricing. They are just dropping the price to get you to sign the contract.

Then the 'Gotcha' comes. Everything seems good for three months, six months or even a year. Then the Chief Financial Officer at the cleaning company starts evaluating the cost/profit breakeven and realizes they aren't making the expected profit from your account.

The next step for your new low cost cleaning company is to cut back staff used on your account and to cut corners on the hours they spend in your business, cleaning.

Why? Because no business, no matter how big can stay in business very long by just cutting prices to get a client.

By now, you are locked in and changing again is just so painful. So you just put up with poor service.

Or, maybe you complain and the service gets better for a month or two. But then it goes back to being the same poor service and you feel stuck.

And what happens, employee morale is affected, customer perception of the quality of your business is affected and ultimately profit is affected.

All for what seemed like a good decision to shave a few dollars off the expense budget.

That's pretty well how this industry works, especially with the top 3 or 4 commercial cleaning companies.

What you should look for the next time you become dissatisfied, is a company that will stop selling you only on price and develop a comprehensive cleaning plan that will give you confidence they know what they are doing.

Chapter 3

Cleaning Crews Have To Be Constantly Reminded

Have you ever had this experience with your cleaning company?

You have an expectation of the areas and steps that need to be taken in the daily and weekly cleaning process, but the cleaning crews frequently miss things.

And it is FRUSTRATING to keep having to remind them to do the standard little things.

Maybe they forget one or two of these (or maybe even more):

- Refilling the toilet paper dispenser rolls.

- Emptying ALL of the trash cans.
- Leaving the bathroom mirrors streaky.
- Cleaning the top of the break room refrigerator. (That thing can get really nasty.)
- Dusting the tops of file cabinets.
- Cleaning the cobwebs out of the corners.
- Leave the bathrooms smelly.
- Waxing the floors properly.
- Or any number of other elements missed.
- Stop moving important documents on the conference room table that you've told them over and over not to do.

You shouldn't have to remind them to do their job. After all you're paying them good money to do the job right.

It's not your job to come behind them and check their work, right?

And you would be exactly right.

Cleaning Companies Should Do Their Own Follow-up

You should only contract with a cleaning company that will demonstrate to you with their in-house procedure manual, that they have a planned and customized follow-up checklist for each cleaning client.

They should demonstrate that this checklist is completed by a management person not already dedicated to that particular cleaning crew.

Here's what often happens. A company may have a checking system. But the person responsible for checking and ensuring that everything was completed is a member of the crew doing the cleaning.

What is the likelihood this person might get busy or lazy and not do a good job of the checking process?

Your time is very valuable. It contributes heavily to the profitability of your company, practice, store or restaurant.

You SHOULD NOT have to constantly follow-up and check behind these people to make sure they are doing their job right.

That SHOULD be the cleaning company's responsibility.

But seldom will you find cleaning companies that will invest in extra staff to double check the work that is done each day or night.

If you invested in a cleaning company that provided the right level of staffing, even if it was a little more money, wouldn't that be a good investment?

Isn't your time far more valuable getting more things done for your company rather than wasting time checking up on your cleaning company?

Be sure your cleaning company commits to you in writing that they will always have a non-crew manager or supervisor who is coming behind the crew and making sure everything is done right.

Chapter 4

They Refuse To Do Special Cleaning

You've seen the scene in a movie or a television program when a couple is interviewing a cleaning lady for their home.

Everything is going great until the new cleaning lady emphatically states, "I don't do windows."

That happens all too often in the commercial cleaning business.

In fact, my company, Bright Star Cleaning often gets special requests to go in and do cleaning jobs others refuse to tackle.

Sometimes that even creates a reason for that company to switch to our full time cleaning services.

There are a lot of strange things that can come up that need cleaning that aren't part of the normal cleaning process.

Christopher Banner

Here are some examples from our customers that we took care of as a normal (or not so normal) part of our services.

Something like this could happen to your company or office. You will want a company that happily takes care of these things for you rather than putting you off.

Example 1:

There was a food chain in town that we were regularly cleaning their facility. I won't mention their name for reasons that will soon be obvious.

One day they came to us with a problem.

One night an employee was working late when everyone was gone and it was quite.

All of a sudden she heard the little feet of animals running across the top of the drop down ooiling tiles. It creeped her out and she closed up and went home immediately.

The next day, the owner called out an exterminator to determine what was the cause.

It turned out the little running feet belonged to a whole nest of mice that had migrated in from the recently vacated business next door.

And, it also turned out they had been up there for quite awhile creating nests and lots and lots of leave behind droppings.

What a mess.

They called us and we said, "Of course we can clean that up."

Most cleaning companies would have told this company, "we don't do windows" or in this case "we don't do mouse droppings".

We immediately went to work clearing out everything left behind by the little hardworking rodents. And not only that, after the cleaning we used our proprietary sanitizing process to make sure the place was totally clean from all potential germ infestation.

Example 2:

One of our clients owns an office building with multiple tenants. One day we received an urgent call.

One of our tenants office is infected with Scabies. The firm's employees were being bitten by the microscopic scabies mites that were living in the carpet, furniture and window coverings.

We immediately responded with our Super-Heated Cleaning Systems. Our high tech equipment immediately destroyed the mites and extracted all of their eggs. That way there was no returning outbreak when the new larvae hatched out in a few days.

You may say, "that will never happen in our offices." But who knows.

You should make sure the cleaning company you choose has a plan for unusual circumstances like this.

If it can happen to our client, it CAN happen to anyone.

Example 3:

This one could be a little unsettling, but if you have a medical practice of any kind, maybe it could happen to you.

A medical practice we clean every day, was seeing one of their elderly patients for a routine exam. The patient was reclined on an examination table waiting on the doctor to come in.

Sadly before the doctor arrived the patient suddenly died on the examining table.

When that happens, bodily fluids are released as the body stops functioning.

This created a big biological mess all over the table and floor. We were called in to disinfect and clean everything. We even had to completely disassemble the examination table to clean all of the fluid remains from the inner workings of the equipment.

This is a sad story. But my question is if you have a medical facility and something happened, would your cleaning company go all out for you to do a truly deep cleaning of equipment and everything.

Not only that, do they have the expertise to make it medically safe again.

Example 4:

One of our clients had a continuing problem with their light fixtures.

They had hanging light fixtures all throughout their facility.

Bugs were getting into the fixtures, dying and laying there in the glass fixtures underneath the bulbs. It was extremely unsightly to their patients.

Almost every week they were having to pay extra to have the units disassembled and cleaned of the dead bugs.

As I alluded to in Chapter 1, to reduce their cost and to speed up the cleaning process, our staff invented a special cleaning tool and system to remove the dead bugs.

This made it faster, easier and less expense for the client. Now THAT is using innovation to reduce the cost of cleaning.

We have now filed a patent application for this device and are waiting on approval.

What's The Message Here

Funny you should ask. Hiring a competent, quality cleaning company isn't just about vacuuming and dusting.

There are many other application that you may need your cleaning company to accomplish.

Be sure you have one that is willing to say YES to any cleaning challenge and has the experience and systems to accomplish the task.

Chapter 5

Just Want To Get Finished As Soon As Possible

Most cleaning company staff members are not motivated to do an outstanding job of cleaning your offices. It's just not in their nature.

Many cleaning companies provide such poor pay to their cleaning staff personnel that they just don't care about how good a job they do on your offices.

Helping Put A Man On The Moon

There is a story that has circulated for many years about President John Kennedy.

During a visit to the NASA space center in 1962, President Kennedy noticed a janitor carrying a broom. He interrupted his tour, walked over to the man and said, "Hi, I'm Jack Kennedy. What are you doing?"

Christopher Banner

"Well, Mr. President," the janitor responded, "I'm helping put a man on the moon."

To most people, this janitor was just cleaning the building. But in the more mythic, larger story unfolding around him, he was helping to make history.

Here's the point: No matter how large or small your role of an employee, they are contributing to the larger story unfolding within your business.

And when that larger story is embraced all the way down to yes, even the cleaning crew, incredible things happen.

You should always have a cleaning company that finds ways to reward their employees and give them a greater purpose in life than just cleaning toilets.

The problem in this industry lies in the lack of appreciation for the value of the employees that are doing the cleaning, the lack of training and the lack of the bigger picture.

Chapter 6

Little Or No Ongoing Dialogue With The Client

Here's a problem that I often find going on when I am talking to a new potential client.

The person responsible for hiring and overseeing the cleaning company feels like the cleaning company doesn't care about the ongoing concerns.

This happens because when many of the companies get a client they begin to take them for granted.

The cleaning company doesn't regularly check in with the onsite contact to make sure their expectations are being met.

Once they get the contract, no one in management of the cleaning company ever seems interested in what the client's needs or concerns are.

Christopher Banner

When was the last time the owner or a senior manager of the cleaning company comes by to check on your satisfaction with their service.

They usually leave this up to the lead person on the cleaning crew.

However, seldom is the client in the offices when the cleaning crews are there. SO, there is little or no interaction.

And worse than that, the cleaning crew is not trained to have the skill to meet with clients and make sure their needs are being met.

As a client, you have a right to have someone come by regularly, when it is convenient for you, to discuss your satisfaction with the service and identify any new needs.

Chapter 7

Random Cleaning Rather Than Systematic Cleaning

Often, cleaning companies hire janitorial staff and give them very little training. After all, anyone should be able to vacuum, dust and clean toilets, right?

But here is what often happens. The cleaning company employee comes in with their own way of doing things.

They start with the cleaning part they like to do and leave the less desirable things till last.

And you know this intuitively. The elements that get left to last get the least attention to detail.

Christopher Banner

When you interview any cleaning company as a potential vendor, you want to make sure they can show you their systematic cleaning system.

Random cleaning will always lead to inferior outcomes.

Systematic cleaning will insure your facility is cleaned properly and completely.

Without a written systematic cleaning process, critical areas will be missed.

Because we live in New Mexico there is a certain order in which your office or facility should be cleaned. For instance. We have lots of wind in New Mexico.

As a result, there is almost always a layer of dust that collects on everything in the office. And our dust isn't nice little friendly dust bunnies.

Our dust has fine grains of sand and dirt that blows in from the desert mesas all around Albuquerque. It is in the air everywhere, constantly. And it is unseen.

UNTIL, it lands on your office furniture, computers, printers, etc. If you just wipe it off with a typical cloth, you can grind those tiny little destructive sand particles into your beautiful expensive furniture and computers.

A quality cleaning company will have a written procedure they systematically adhere to where they dust first. By doing this with the proper dusting devices, they will move those particles to the floor where they can be removed with the high velocity floor cleaning system.

That's another problem here. Most cleaning companies just use standard old everyday vacuum cleaners for the carpets.

You want to make sure your cleaning company had special systems that prevent all of those tiny sand particles from being catapulted back out into the air.

There is always an exhaust system on all vacuum cleaners. Is your company using a patented clean and capture system to make sure the air is clean after they finish?

Here are some areas that are often missed because there is no systematic written system for cleaning.

- Chairs are not moved and under desks vacuumed.
- No systematic plan for vacuuming. They only vacuum where there is visible dirt. They miss the other areas.
- Areas behind doors are often overlooked. When you don't vacuum and clean these, there is a buildup that migrates to other parts of the office. And it can be embarrassing when you close the door for a private meeting with a client or vendor.
- Many things are missed in dusting. Picture frames, the tops of door molding, high ledges, tops of cabinets, etc. are frequently missed. Left uncleaned, this can cause allergies to develop in you and your employees. That can cause loss of focus by employees and errors that cost your business money.
- Interior glass can be missed and left hazy for days or weeks giving a false impression of the quality of your business.

You will always want to make sure your cleaning company can show you their written system for cleaning your facility.

Conclusion

The cleanliness of your facility should not be something you have to constantly supervise or worry about.

A quality cleaning company will be able to demonstrate the systems, specialized equipment and patented processes they use to make sure your workplace does not hamper the efficiency of your workforce.

Few business owners and senior managers are aware of the significant impact a properly cleaned workplace has on the efficiency of the employees and management.

We have seen instance after instance where a company's efficiency was being affected when improper cleaning allowed for the excess spreading of viral infections, colds and harmful germs.

That means more downtime of employees and employees not working at top efficiency. When that happens the business suffers and the profit drops.

Sadly, there are many ways cleaning companies shortcut and provide less than stellar service to their clients.

You can avoid that by insisting they show you their systematic cleaning plan and demonstrate how they insure that it is adhered to each and every day of cleaning.

Request Your Systematic Cleaning Analysis

If you feel your current cleaning service is not providing the service you deserve, and your money is being wasted, you should review that service and consider changing.

Bright Star Cleaning offers a Free "15 Step Cleaning Analysis" to help you evaluate your needs and create a spic and span clean office to improve employee morale and health.

You deserve to have a showcase office for your clients, customers, or patients.

In fact your satisfaction is so important to us that we make a pledge to you by giving your our "Office Cleaning Bill of Rights" found on the next page.

Call us on
505.900.3535
To Schedule Your Analysis

Your Bright Star Cleaning
BILL OF RIGHTS

As a Bright Star Cleaning Customer:

1. You have the right to a thoroughly clean, hygienic and safe facility.
2. You have the right to have any queries or concerns answered promptly, any time, day or night, when you call our special customer only hotline 505-263-4398.
3. You have the right to have any of your service needs addressed within 2 hours of placing your call.
4. You have the right to open and frequent communication from Bright Star staff on any topic or issue.
5. You have the right to always expect us to perform the services agreed upon in our Agreement even after the first few months or the first year. GUARANTEED.
6. You have the right to expect to see Bright Star Cleaning staff who are courteous and professionally dressed at all times.
7. You have a right to expect Bright Star to only utilize professional, high quality products and processes when cleaning your facility.
8. You have the right to expect us to perform the agreed upon services within the allocated time window initially identified.
9. You have the right to expect us to do the job right the first time, or we will do it over, at no charge.
10. You have the right to expect a full refund or credit, if your first month's Cleaning does not blow you away and exceed your expectations.

Additional Information

For more information about the change in cleaning experience you deserve when Bright Star Cleaning is your professional cleaning service and to receive your comprehensive 15 step cleaning analysis, please contact us at:

505.900.3535

Bright Star Cleaning

6020 B Midway Park

Albuquerque, NM 87109

www.ingramcontent.com/pod-product-compliance
Lightning Source LLC
Chambersburg PA
CBHW071436200326
41520CB00014B/3717